Allen's Poetry

Book I

The Early Years

D. Allen Cohen

Reproductions of any of the contents of this book for commercial purposes, without the written permission of the author or his legal representative, are prohibited.

Cover design quilt created by Phyllis L Cohen.

Copyright © 2013 D. Allen Cohen

All rights reserved.

ISBN-10: 0615795544
ISBN-13: 978-0615795546
Phainopepla Publishing

DEDICATION

Poetry runs in the family. Perhaps there is a poetry gene or virus. To start with, both my mother, Faye, and her sister, Elizabeth, were poets:

>Here I sit
>On top of the Totem Pole of my Family Tree
>No Parent left
>To spread protective, loving wings over me –
>Their child ... – Faye

>Thoughts are born on gossamer wings
>Through vortex of fantastic things
>Whirling and dancing in joy supreme
>   Strange --- enchanting, as in a dream – Elizabeth

Phyllis, my wife, my love, writes the most delightful poetry. From our Kenya adventure:

>Topi on the hill
>Cheetah on the kill
>Run baby run
>Run baby run

>Sand castles reaching to the sky
>Home to creatures littler than I

>Peck, peck, nibble
>Needle, spindle, chug
>Fight, bite, swallow
>Juicy, hairy bug

Our daughter, Nicki inherited the gene and her husband, Ken has his own family poetry gene:

> Dear Mom
> To one who rocked me and talked to me
> Fed me and changed me
> Raised me
> And gave me away in marriage
> I give – with my husband
> To you and my father
> Our son, to be your grandson – Nicki
>
> I thought of you this morning, my son
> As I passed by the lace of snow frosted branches
> The white web replacing the fallen green-turned-to-colour leaves from ever-so-long a season ago …– Ken

The poetry gene reappeared in the next generation in Mark and Kathy's children, Michael and Rachel (14):

> Creation! Oh what is your source?
> That origin of your flowing force
> What spirits doth create the Muse?
> Whose clarion call I can't refuse – Michael
>
> Monkshood, Columbine, and Tuberous Begonia
> Angel's Trumpet, Camellia, Chrysanthemum and Fuchsia
> Through a tall red entrance, down steps, mazes and streams
> We enter a Japanese Garden favoured by sun's beams – Rachel M

Also Nicki and Ken's daughters, Ilana (age 7?) and Sarit (15):

> Dreams are images in your head
> You have them in school and when you're in bed
> Dreams can be good or dreams can be bad
> Or sometimes you can have dreams quite sad - Ilana

Now over the ocean, and to a new land
On the way many orcas are close at hand
Their tails above water, their bodies below
Just a glimpse of their beauty, then under they go – Sarit

Also Kathy:

> Living life in his own way
> Creating his strengths
> His happiness
> Strong positive beliefs
> An attitude that makes you say
> We're proud of you, Dad

My niece, Rachel Ann appears to have inherited the poetry gene as well:

> Essence of Gaia, Freya and Danu
> mothers, nurtures all
> celebrating life in the embrace of family
> cherishing children and surrendering self
>
> Phyllis, Essence of Love – Rachel Ann

I am both humbled and thrilled by this genetic poetic DNA strain that runs through the family. I'm sure there are some closet poets in the family as well. May the poetry gene continue to flourish in the family for generations. I therefore dedicate these volumes to all the family poets and to all who have inspired the poetry herein. Please continue composing.

TABLE OF CONTENTS

Dedication.. 2
Introduction to All Three Books... 7
Introduction to Book I, "The Early Years"............................. 9
Poems:
      Occasions I: Happenings, Tributes, Humor................ 10
      My Love I... 39
      Spiritual I: Loss, On God 55
      Commentary I: Observations, Philosophy, Politics, Places
      62
      Epic I: That Mobile Abode, Ode to a Squaw Dress,
      Song of the Maccabee... 97
Introduction to Book II, "The Middle Years"........................... 117
Introduction to Book III, "The Later Years"............................. 118

INTRODUCTION TO ALL THREE BOOKS

Who would want to read a book of poetry authored by, as a poet, an unknown? A typical comment I would expect is: "Oh that's nice." So what makes me think you will want to read these books? Well, for one thing, you might find yourself among the poems. Or even better, you might see yourself from a different perspective, or find an opinion with which you can take issue. I don't write "Oh that's nice" poetry; at least I try not to. Some things I've written, like the adventures of Pa Poke (Book II), you may think of as a bit farfetched, but never fluffy of stuffy.

I have learned from the masters: depth of feeling, rhythm and rhyme from V. Lindsay and E.A. Poe; passion, longing and emotion from E.B. Browning and Lord and Lady Byron; compassion, memories, reverence, loss and grief from A. Pope, W. Wordsworth and A Lincoln; story-telling from H.W. Longfellow and E. L. Thayer; humor from E. W. Lord and E. V. Cooke; tall, and not-so- tall tales and adventure from R. W. Service, A. Tennyson and C. F. Woolson; ... and so much and so many more. I am truly in their debt.

However, although I may borrow a rhythm or rhyme scheme, my poetry is mine and speaks of you and to you. It also speaks to me while leaving me a bit unclothed and inwardly revealed. I began writing poetry when I was thirteen. Mrs. Sullivan, a marvelous teacher, challenged each of us in her English class to write a Shakespearian sonnet. I did:

By chance a glance I threw the velvet night ... (page 11).

I was told years later by a teacher cousin of mine that Mrs. Sullivan had apparently submitted the poem to an anthology of children's poetry and that it was accepted and published.

These three volumes are organized by time periods: Book I – Early Years (around 1963 and earlier), Book II – Middle Years (1964 to 1999) and Book III – Later Years (2000 to the date of publication). Within each volume the poems are arranged by category (Occasions, My Love, Spiritual, Commentary and Epic) and within each category, approximately by date. For many of the earlier poems the date is guestimated.

Phyllis and I have constructed an index of names (only first names and initials) together with the page numbers of poems referencing the names (see Book III). Also, I have written some brief introductory recollections about the poems or groups of poems to help place them in context.

As of July this year (2013) Phyllis and I will have been married for 60 years, and I will have completed my 80th (for Phyllis, somewhat fewer). We see these volumes as one way of thankfully expressing all the fullness of life we have known.

INTRODUCTION TO BOOK I, THE EARLY YEARS
1946 TO 1963

This period includes Amphitheater High School, The University of Arizona, marriage, young children, graduate school and the US Air Force. Places include Tucson, Arizona; Cleveland, Ohio; Dayton, Ohio and Colorado Springs, Colorado.

Many of these poems were originally collected in a hand-written, mimeographed book that Phyllis and I put together for the family in 1956 while I was a graduate student at Case Institute of Technology in Cleveland. By that time Nicki and Mark had joined the family and we were living in a high-rise, public-housing apartment in down-town Cleveland. We titled the book, "Patches". In addition to the poetry, I had made simple sketches to accompany the poetry. I have included some of those sketches here close to their associated poems and elsewhere throughout the 3 books.

In general this was a period of discovery, discovering each other as a young couple, a young family in new environments, and new (to us) ideas and challenges.

OCCASIONS I

"Occasions I" includes 30 poems ranging from 1946 to 1963. Thirteen of these are from the book, "Patches" referenced in the introduction. Through these poems I glimpse the feelings of a young couple, struggling to raise a family, to keep food on the table while preparing for an uncertain but hopeful future. Most of the poems are family oriented toward parents, siblings, ourselves and our newly minted children.

Shooting Star is the Shakespearian sonnet mentioned earlier (page 7). In case you don't remember, a normal sonnet has 14 iambic-pentameter lines with the rhyme scheme: ABAB CDCD EFEF GG, whereas a Shakespearian sonnet has the rhyme scheme: ABBA CDDC EFEF GG (according to Mrs. Sullivan).

<u>Shooting Star</u>
D.A.C circa 1946

By chance a glance I threw the velvet night
Expectancy appeared among the stars
I focused on the inky void afar
From whence burst forth a flaming meteorite

It lived but long enough to catch my breath
And yet a life's eternity was there
Its time of brilliance causing me to stare
'Twas born to bloom then fade away to death

For aren't our lives but just an instant's length
In light of Him who is eternity
Our hopes, our fears, our weaknesses and strengths
Are pebbles under cliffs of time to be

I can but wonder at the way things are
How much our lives are like a shooting star

The Ice-Cream Man was my attempt to earn some money by submitting poetry describing N Rockwell's cover paintings for the Saturday Evening Post. They didn't buy it.

The Ice-Cream Man
July, 1954 DAC

Excitement thrills the summer air
As people arrive from everywhere
With picnic baskets filled to the brim
Down at the lake for a mid-day swim

Rear car doors slam 'midst whoops of joy
As rough and tumble little boys
And little girls with eyes that shine
All run ker-splash to the water line

The older folks in beach attire
Just sit and bask, and never tire
Of watching as the children play
Remembering their former days

The afternoon in lazy pace
Meanders on its placid race
Against the evening's cool, fresh airs
With soothing winds to whisk off cares

Then ting-a-ling resounds the lake
As youthful stomachs start to quake
Soon 'cross the lake a raucous noise
As rough and tumble little boys

And little girls with eyes that shine
Come running from the water line
To gather nickels, if they can
Because he's here, the ice-cream man

The day we learned that baby Nicki was on the way, Phyllis' mother, Rose, learned of the death of her father's step mother, Necha, after whom Nicki was named. I wrote her this poem.

Cycle
Patches, February, 1955

Though golden leaves soon turn to dust
The Lord of life fulfills His trust
For in the wake of autumn morn
A tiny baby will be born

My father, Norman, smoked Camel cigarettes constantly, even after the Surgeon General made public the connection between smoking and lung cancer.

The poetry format of Dear Dad I have used often as one of my tongue-in-cheek poetry formats.

<u>Dear Dad</u>
Patches, Early 1955

Speaking now of Vice and Morals
And of daily family quarrels
   Roots and bases
   Boots and faces
There is one thing does stand out
That the basis of the quarrels
   From within and
   From without
One attributes to the wishes
Of the Good and Moral Mother
That the Good and Moral Father
Keep his ashes off the dishes!

Daddy's Day I wrote to my father when he was having a hard time with an early neck injury that had revisited him in his older age. It was my attempt to put a smile on his face, which it did. It turns out that my children really loved this poem and fed it back to me a number of Father's Days since.

Daddy's Day
Patches, June, 1954 or 1955

Some things is dad-burned hard to say
'Cause I ain't never talked that way
But I'm gonna wish you anyway
A ding dong dandy Daddy's Day!

I don't recall what occasion or situation prompted Family Elders, which is one of a number of poems I wrote to my mother, Faye. Since Faye was quite a poet and received the "Golden Poet Award, 1989" from the World of Poetry organization, we would often exchange poems back and forth.

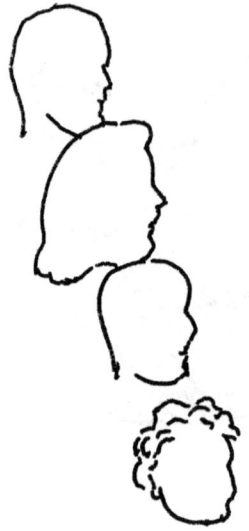

<u>Family Elders</u>
Patches, 1956

So few are those who understand
True depth and true emotion
As visioned in a Mother's eye
With faith and pure devotion
And those of generations past
Those mothers of mothers of sons
Are cherished most by offspring hence
Whose heritage they have gained

This is another example of me, in my youth, trying to understand the mother, son relationship. I don't know that my mother really "led the way" or even that I thought she did back then, but it sounded good.

<u>From Your Son</u>
Patches, Early, 1950s

I woke from out an unborn fantasy
And found myself beneath a lofty hill
I felt your soul reach out and say to me
      "Arise my son
      Your hill is one
Do with it what you will."

With faltering steps I started up the trail
My motion gained momentum as I went
And ever when by chance my feet should fail
      You spurred me on
      And fear was gone
And pathways soon unbent

I stand now at the brink of manlihood
And yet my summit is as far away
As it was then, when at the base I stood
      My peak is set
      But it climbs yet
With you leading the way

D. Allen Cohen

While I was still in high school, in the civics class we studied WWI and WWII the latter having just recently come to an end. This prompted the following poem a year or so later.

<u>Lucifer 1922 – 1952</u>
Patches, 1952

Was once I dwelt within a worldly eve
And listened while the calm revealed to me
    An artificial core of quietude
    Complacency, indifferent attitude
And yet within this false serenity
A breath of danger spoke eternity
    But not a bough bent to the warning breeze
    The still had smothered infant memories

'Twas then a bolt of fear I cast on thee
Which fell a multitude of lofty trees
    Complacency begot depression's scorn
    And so to soothe thy burns I wrought thee storm
I slyly let the rain to reign supreme
And gave it hail to bolster its esteem
    Its prejudicial flood choked half the Earth
    Before the other half renounced its worth

An eagle built a windmill in the sky
And wind's own fury rendered waters dry
    The storm was spent within a week of years
    And dead leaves drifted off in streams of tears
Then from two seeds that I sowed deep in thee
Grew two great weeds who worked in harmony
Till on thee, I the fuel of fear dispatched
Behold me now while I ignite the match

My brother, Marvin (older by 1½ years) loved to use fifty-cent words, whereas mine were more like nickels. So, when he turned 21, the legal drinking age in Arizona, I wrote him the following.

Dear Marvin
Patches, October 16, 1952

In discoursing 'round imbibing
Now that you are twenty one
I'll endeavor to synopsis
Connotations overdone
    Reputation's implications
    From your rations estimations
    In ichthyic bibulation
Would undoubtedly conclude
That the championship you've won

This was also written to Marvin when he and his wife, Frances purchased their first automobile.

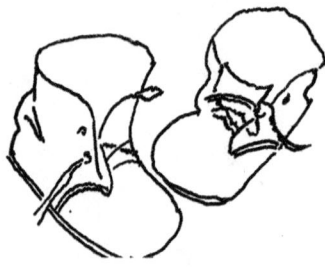

<u>Ode to a Dodge Pair of Shoes</u>
Patches, 1956

In most circumstances
Those low in finances
Begin with the Old –
Then the New

But some individuals
With money residuals
The size of a
Large drop of dew

Feel life has unfurled
They leap for the world
And land in a hot
Pot of stew

But in circumstances
A few little chances
Let's say – like a new
Pair of shoes

Can be reconciled
Just don't go hog wild
And don't dent that new
Pair of shoes

Nicki Jean was born just before I was scheduled to leave for Cleveland, Ohio to start graduate school. Phyllis and Nicki flew to join me in Cleveland when Nicki was 3 weeks old. The flight required changing planes in Chicago. This was Phyllis' (and Nicki's) first flight. Phyllis never let go of the baby for the whole time. You can imagine the state she was in when she finally arrived.

<u>Nicki Jean Born in a Jiffy</u>
September, 1955

The first of September in fifty five
At ten before three in the morning
A dear little blessing to Phyllis and me
Had broadcast forth her virgin plea
Heard 'round the world there announcing
That wee Nicki Jean did arrive

Now, Nicki Jean came in the nick of time
When all were around to behold
For Marvin and Fran had arrived to stay
And I was leaving the very next day
So when in the future this story is told
We'll remember this blessing sublime

<u>A Cutie</u>
January, 1956

We know Nicki baby's a cutie
And dressing her well is our duty
Though some things are dearer
It takes fifty lira
To keep baby Nicki in booties

Sam, Marv and Fran's first, was born shortly after Nicki was born. Like Nicki, he was delivered at Tucson Medical Center by the same doctor

<u>Samuel David</u>
November, 1956

Summon the Funsters
Rally the band
Heart of a youngster
Felt 'cross the land
Once he was infant
Time gone astray
Boyhood triumphant
One year today

Although I had had several flying lessons at a post-war, Veteran's-Administration supported flying school, working 4 hours for 1 hour of flying time; I had not been on a commercial airliner until I flew from Tucson to New Jersey on Fort Huachuca (where I was working for the summer) business. I was enthralled by the experience.

<u>In Flight</u>
Patches, September, 1955

Flit by you messengers of the wind
So fluffy white
Now here
Now there
So nonchalantly dancing on our silvery wings

How come you by your merriment
Like downy elves with hidden wings
Bemused at our robotic bird
That dares defy your playful solitude

Like you we too can fly

One doesn't often realize how wise one's parents were until you become one.

<u>Of Parents of Children</u>
Patches, 1956

Now that I have entered parenthood
The wisdom of your guidance through my youth
Has clarified itself in all its truth
I hope that I may somehow be as good

During one period of my youth I did not fully appreciate the finer qualities of my father. I saw only what I perceived as his weaknesses. I wrote this poem but never gave it to him. He did not see it until he read Patches. I suspect that he suspected that it referred to him but he never questioned me on it.

Tipsy Towers
Patches, Early 1950s

It's true you lived in foolish youth
Not having values set
Your weakness pampered you to truth
Allowing to forget
The hum-drum tedium of life

You built your castles tissue thin
With tipsy towers to live within
With gates that never fail to swing
With nightingales that always sing

Though thorns encroached your liberty
And scratched reality
You bathed yourself in sympathy
Determined not to be
Perpetually perturbed by life

Then thunder clouds began to rain
And tipsy towers caved in on pain
And gates were warped beyond their shape
You woozy world was rent in rape

And now the pain's unbearable
Still sympathy you seek
The teasing time to terrible
To woo the wretched weak
And issue them their souls from life

So build your castles now in brick
And wall your tipsy towers thick
'Though pain remains forever near
Involve resolve to persevere

Oh well, no comment!

<u>What's The Matter?</u>
Patches, Circa 1956

In the course of matters normal
Certain things, 'though quite informal
      Seem to muster
      Such a bluster
That the whole house does resound

Of these matters most disastrous
      Most of most
      That can be found
It's the matter in the morning
When the calm, collected Father
Gives the lavatory walls
A calm, collected kick
'Cause the razor in his hand
Chipped his chin a little nick

This poem brings back those delicious emotions that I felt on the occasion of the first birthday of my first child.

<u>My Little One</u>
September 1, 1956
Patches

Then how can I describe with flimsy words
That winsome wisp of femininity
Who dwells in infantile mimicry
Appearing all so pleasingly absurd

So delicately clumsy, little one –
So funny face, so infinitely pure
Such gibberish, what meanings to infer
So beautifully you, my little one

A baby is a baby not for long
But as you wean away your childhood nest
And find the place in life where you belong
A fragment will remain within my breast

Of curly hair, and eyes so full of fun
Of you, my little one when you were one

Phyllis' second Mommy's Day was special since she received her first poem from her daughter (with a little help from me).

<u>Mommy's Day</u>
May, 1957

Dear Mommy, though I cannot write
And say the things I feel so deep
I've asked my daddy if he might
Write down just what you mean to me

I know I'm not a perfect child
And seldom do just what you say –
The times I nearly run you wild
Or don't come in when called from play

But, Mommy, I am only me
And though I'm awfully, awfully smart
I cannot see as parents see
I only do what's in my heart

So, Mommy, you are everything
And though I try my very best
I need what only you can bring
The love that lies within your breast

And Mommy, I would like to say
A very happy Mommy's Day

And then to my mom ...

Mother's Day
May, 1957

Dear Mom

These words that come to you today
Bear all the depth within my heart
My most affection they impart
Dear Mom, a happy Mother's Day

My thoughts are not just of today
Nor just the years that we're apart
My love goes back beyond the start
Dear Mom, a happy Mother's Day

I gave Phyllis a present on that Mother's Day, but she had first to solve the following riddle. Can you solve it?

Riddle
May, 1957

Is there such a thing
That neither gurgles, crawls, nor cries
That's either soaking wet or dry
That covers 'round a water spout,
Which runs a while and then goes out
That shocks you with an open end
When sudden currents it may send
One should not be without this thing
What funny present do I bring?

D. Allen Cohen

In 1957 we moved to Wright Patterson Air Force Base near Dayton, Ohio after I had received my Master's diploma. I was a newly commissioned 2nd Lieutenant. Shortly after settling in, an event took place that even today shakes me up a bit to remember it.

<u>A Day of Days</u>
Wright Patterson Air Force Base
September 24, 1957

The air of evening glistened cool
A day of days like every day
The clatter of the neighborhood
That echoes whines of passing jets
And rumbles with a bomber's roar
Could not forewarn of tragedy
Could not escape the sigh of death

Machine of myriad moving parts
With human hands to guide its frame
A takeoff for a routine flight
A final solemn plunge to death

Now spins the human roulette wheel
Where Death plays solitaire with Time
The shadow of this silver bird
Arousing terror in its wake
Rejoins its master's crippled frame
In metal, flame and flesh

The Lord accepts four human souls
And statisticians make their mark
The clatter of the neighborhood
Still echoes whines of passing jets
And rumbles with a bomber's roar
A day of days like every day

This poem is a continuation of my probing into the mother-child relationship as I observed it in myself and was witnessing it in my children.

Mother – Child
Circa 1958

Some concepts are too delicate to voice
Though thoughts do come to prey upon my tongue
No words will flow
But pen in hand makes bold these silent words
And echoes forth the passion of their source
The mind, the soul

A child is raised with tender care and warmth
But in this maturation phase
A child is tossed from love to hate
And back again to love
Directed toward the tap roots of his birth
And in this tender age is cast the die
To guide him through the morals of his life

An Oedipus is born with every birth
To suckle fondly at his mother's breast
And to each man the Sphinx of mother love
Remains a mystery remnant of his past

The ramblings of these lines may seem obscure
But so is the relationship that's shared
Born of pain and joy of birth
Maternal love matured by years and taste

Dale was born at Fort Carson, Colorado while I was a newly degreed PhD, Instructor and 1st Lieutenant at the Air Force Academy.

Phyllis Would A Mother Be
October 20, 1960

Phyllis would a mother be
For having fun with her honey
Phyllis would a mother be
She bore sweet Nicki Jean for me
With a hey and a hi and a fiddle dee dee
For having fun with her honey

Phyllis would a mother be
While having not enough money
Phyllis would a mother be
And Mark she bounced upon my knee
With a hey and a hi and a fiddle dee dee
While having not enough money

Phyllis would a mother be
The days of Summer were sunny
Phyllis would a mother be
Then August saw me rocking Lee
With a hey and a hi and a fiddle dee dee
The days of Summer were sunny

Phyllis would a mother be
The next verse may not be any
Phyllis would a mother be
Dale Charles joined the other three
With a hey and a hi and a fiddle dee dee
For having more is too many

I wrote poems about Mark, Lee and Dale when they were born and thereafter, but they somehow were lost in our wanderings as a family over the past 50 years or so. The following is the earliest poem about Mark that I could find.

<u>My Boy, Mark</u>
Age 5
May 1, 1962

My Boy – and how shall I describe him –
Not in whimsical refrains
But in brash and boyish strains
Such as trucks and tops
And lollypops
A panda bear
A broken chair
All these – and yet they can't describe him
There is something in his way
An intangible display
That is mirrored in the sparkle of his eyes
A buffoon for all to see –
And they say he looks like me
Is he just a little daddy in disguise?
Soon he'll don the mask of years
And embrace a world of fears
To exchange his truck and teddy for a gun
But this vintage memory
Will restore my boy to me
Bright and carefree spirit of his father's son

D. Allen Cohen

With apologies to HMS Pinafore, upon five of us lieutenants achieving the rank of temporary-captain, I wrote this song for all of us to sing at the dining-in honoring the occasion.

Newly Ranking Captains We
(To the tune of "When I was a Lad")
October, 1963

When we were lieutenants we served our time
Doing silly little projects that were far from prime
We treated our superiors in proper form
And saluted everything that wore a uniform

We saluted everybody so snappily
That newly ranking Captains in the Force are we
We saluted everybody so snappily
That newly ranking Captains in the Force are we

We suffered all the functions that were protocol
And assured each hostess hers' was best of all
Our wives were so charming, our pride did swell
In the art of entertaining they did excel.

They entertained the people so properly
That newly ranking Captains in the Force are we
They entertained the people so properly
That newly ranking Captains in the Force are we

In sports with superiors competed we
As we fiercely fought their way to victory
Whether on the squash court or the putting green
We'd put up the biggest battle you have ever seen

> We put up the biggest battle so properly
> That newly ranking Captains in the Force are we
> We put up the biggest battle so properly
> That newly ranking Captains in the Force are we

When asked for opinions in our specialty
We would ponder the problems most judiciously
We would figure what the ranking thought would be
Then forthright and honestly would we agree

> We gave our opinions so properly
> That newly ranking Captains in the Force are we
> We gave our opinions so properly
> That newly ranking Captains in the Force are we

And now that we're Captains with our bars of two
We have gained the recognition that we feel is due
And in the future we will try our best
To continue on the road that led 'to this success

> And if we do this properly
> Then newly ranking Majors in the Force we'll be
> And if we do this properly
> Then newly ranking Majors in the Force we'll be

While at the Air Force Academy another officer, whose baby daughter had leukemia, and I formed the Pikes Peak Chapter of the Leukemia Society to raise research funds. During this period his wife gave birth to a second daughter, Lisa Ann. I composed this lullaby for her.

<u>To Lisa Ann, a Lullaby</u>
Circa 1963

The infant rocks the World to sleep
And suckles on its memories – bare breasted life
May life be yours
May love be yours
May light and beauty shine your eyes
May grace betake your word and ways
And sorrow leave you wise

To soon
The world awakes
The cleavage spanned
The mist of Eden gone
So nestle deep
Your mother's love
And grow, sweet Lisa Ann

The following two poems describe Mark and Lee on the occasions of their sixth and fifth birthdays, respectively.

Hi Mark, Age 6
May 1, 1963

Hi Mark!
    A boy so big, a sheepish grin
    His pockets full of hands and things
What are you doing?
    A dimple of dust across his chin
    Blue eyes the light of boyhood brings
You say it's your birthday?
    All scuff and tough, all soft and warm
    The melody of a sapling lad
Six years old!
    The world to him his mother's arms
    He lives the likeness of his dad
Happy Birthday, Mark!

The Sabbath, My Son
To Lee, Age 5
August 1, 1963

His eyes
    Are most obvious
    Iridescent windows of tomorrow's man
    The glow of candle's Sabbath light
His mind
    Is most subtle
    Honing sparks of logic fresh and unconstrained
    The yeast of wisdom's Sabbath bread
His name
    Is Lee Michael
    Delicately seasoned love and love of life
    Tomorrows cup of Sabbath wine

Marvin B was a dear grad-school friend. We used to exchange silly poems such as these that I wrote him after a visit (my last) while at the AF Academy.

<u>Flojito</u>
To Marv B
Circa May, 1963

Fair thee fond, my friendly well
Undergone, I, yonder hell
Cry thee laughter in your beer
Kindle knowledge in your tear

Yestermorrow dim and dawn
Of the here and never gone
Ultimeet we timely then
Singing songly drinks again

Also, to Marvin B, mi amigo.

Un temprano momentito
Fue' hacido un flojito
Pelo ralo, rojojito
Con un seso tan poquito

MY LOVE I

This includes 16 poems ranging from 1946 to 1963. Eight of these are from the book, "Patches" referenced in the introduction.

Phyllis and I will have been married for at least 60 years by the time you are reading this. Although times have been difficult as well as good, we as individuals, our mutual respect for each other, as well as our love for each other have grown and matured over the years. I can see this in the MY LOVE poems of this and those of the following two books. Perhaps they constitute something of a recipe.

My cousin, Shirley introduced the two of us at a University of Arizona Hillel Foundation function in September of 1952. One of our first dates began with my attendance at her graduation from Tucson High School. As an element of my gift to her (and my first poem to her), I wrote her the following (tongue in cheek, of course!) on a diaper. However, in spite of this we did continue dating.

<u>My High School Graduation Story</u>
Patches, To Phyllis: June, 1952

Now when Ah was a young-un
About the age of three
Mah Mammy sat me on a stool
An' thar she said to me,
"Now honey, listen to me close,
Obey the Golden Rule,
Keep yo' chin up high
An yo' diaper dry
An yo'll do well in school"

Now when Ah was a young-un
About the age of six
May mammy traipsed me off to school
Which got me in a fix
Ah met some fellers 'round the bend
Who said Ah were a fool
With mah chin up high
An' mah diaper dry
Ah marched right into school

Now when Ah was a young-un
About the grade of eight
Mah Mammy said, "Now hurry up
Or else yo sho be late"
So up Ah ran where a fella shoved
A diploma in my han'
With my chin up high
An' mah diaper dry
Ah said, "Ah thank yo man!"

Now when Ah weren't no young-un
But not quite old enough
A feller took me on a date
Ta show me stars an' stuff
He ran his fingers through mah hair
An' puckered up real wide
With mah chin up high
'An mah diaper dry
I turned an' ran inside

Now when Ah weren't much older
But wiser then by far
A fella took me on a walk
But not to look at stars
Now when he kissed me on mah lips
Ah said Ah were a fool
With mah chin up high
'An mah diaper dry
Ah haint learned that in school

So now Ah haint no young-un
Although mah folks think so
'Cause Ah jist graduated
High school jist aint no mo
But when that fella shook my han'
I got so gol darned keyed
With mah chin up high
Don't ask me why
I jist stood thar an ... !

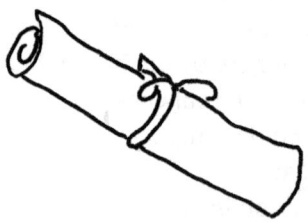

We had planned to be married in the fall of 1953. Right after Phyllis' birthday I was leaving town to work underground in the copper mines of Miami, Arizona next door to Globe. For her birthday, among other things I gave her 3 roses.

<u>Roses a Lady</u>
June 21, 1953
Patches, 1956

Red Rose a lady
Subtle passion
Deep and moody
Flaming fashion
Bathed in beauty

Yellow Rose a lady
Carefree spirit
Gaily dancing
Tender merit
Shy romancing

White Rose a lady
Soft emotion
Dainty lover
Pure devotion
Wife and Mother

As it turns out we were married on July 2nd due to the fact that my grandma Ella had misinterpreted my mother's letter and purchased tickets to be in Tucson July first for the wedding. Phyllis found out on June 29th, called me in Globe, and I hitch-hiked back to Tucson on June 30th. We obtained our marriage license on July 1st and were married the next day.

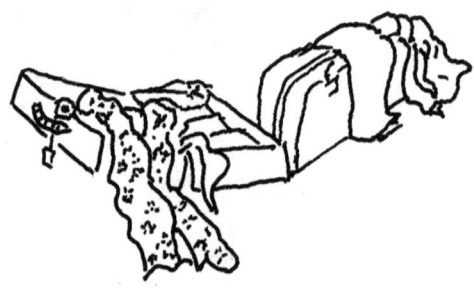

<u>Delightful</u>
Patches, July, 1953

Certain things, 'though quite delightful
At the time appear so frightful
That one shying, almost crying
Starts to balk in bleak despair

Of these pleasures, almost doubtful
For a certain sex so fair

Doubtful most the first night wed
When the husband shyly clothed
Whispers to his sweet betrothed
Come my wife, let's go to bed

I don' recall when I wrote this but I thought it fit in right here.

The Wedding Word
Patches, 1956

It was a rare occasion
For angles, black and white,
To have a celebration
Together through the night
      The Lord decreed
      This lovely deed
And the Devil readily agreed
That for once the Lord was right

It was that Man on Earth,
God's latest recreation,
Should try to prove his worth
And boost the population
      The Lord did cleave
      The Woman Eve
From Goodly Adam who was pleased
So soon they two gave birth

And, too, was born tradition
Or so the story's said
This holy celebration
When man and mate are wed,
      And down the aisle
      God's goodly smile
Is reigning on them all the while,
Till the Devil reigns in bed

Our first residence was in Globe, Arizona while I worked in the copper mines. In a sense it was our honeymoon. The dog referred to in the poem was an almost full sized, stuffed, black Scotty whom we named, Mr. Witherbottom.

<u>Two Months</u>
September 2, 1953

It was then middle summer
When Phi and I were wed
And now two months have near fled by
Since first we went to bed
We tasted sweet that song of life
On love, love, love we fed

It was yet middle summer
When Phi and I were wed
Our heads were in a whirl
Like spinning in a fog
To think they used to tell me
It's like rolling off a log
Well now that I'm experienced
And shouldn't go whole hog
Here's something else to cuddle
A little puppy dog

<u>First Anniversary</u>
July 2, 1954
Patches, 1956

How difficult to find
A word cast in a mist
Haze that lingers in the mind
Expressing what exists
So deep within the soul

My wife, the year is yesterday
A year endowed with ever present thoughts
So near the tongue
In search of phrases to betray
An earnest heart in silent prayer for Love
Unto our final goal

After graduating from the U of A, I took a summer position as an Engineer at Ft. Huachuca, Arizona, living there during the week and returning to Tucson on weekends. While there I finagled a business trip to New Jersey. Being lonely and alone, I wrote the following poem to Phyllis for her birthday.

<u>The Way I Feel</u>
June 20, 1955
From Ft. Monmouth, NJ

How deep can love become on tissue silk

How can man bind his heart and soul and mind
To feel the passion at his finger tips
The longing in his flesh
The quivering of lips
A silent touch
And put them down on paper's silent memory
As messages in ink

It's true this paper cannot see nor smell nor feel
But it can say these words in tones
So soft ... yet clear ... on tissue silk

I love you dear ... my wife ... my own

I believe that this poem was for the occasion of our second anniversary but probably written earlier. We were living on Eastland Street, I had recently completed my senior year at the U of A and Phyllis was working at Levy's Dept. Store.

Recipe
Patches, 1955

Simple is the life we lead
Beautiful the days
Striving toward a distant goal
A hazy goal
Where warmth and light remain
To shed on generations hence

Our marriage in its infancy
Has just begun to wend its rocky way
To family-hood
Though destiny may test our faith
We will achieve that distant day
When hazy ends grow crystal clear
Then generations hence will know
Our marriage in entirety
Was fashioned to the recipe
Of infinite devotion

The following three poems were observations of young married life.

A Wedding Note
Patches, 1956

A family's born in just three little steps –
Two candle sticks to kindle lasting love
A fork and spoon to greet the stork above
A pup to fetch the paper from the steps

Freudian
Patches, 1956

In walks beauty stark and bare
In her shoes and stockings there
"I am free and I can fly
But never catch a cold shall I"

Silent Pair
Patches, 1956

Mother, daughter, silent pair
Breast and baby bonded there
Weak the mighty
Meek the haughty
Shadowed by the love they share

Our third anniversary found us in Cleveland; I had completed my first year of graduate school and Nicki was 10 months old.

My Wife, Third Anniversary
July 2, 1956

So quietly we dwell on Earth
Our unpretentious way
Our bond is not by spoken word
Nor state decree
Though these may be

But in our deep unspoken word
An ember glance
The warmth of flesh
Partaking of creation's act
The taste of flesh
A sacred pact
Our child's birth

D. Allen Cohen

In 1960 I received my doctorate in physics from Case Institute after which we moved to the Air Force Academy north of Colorado Springs, Colorado where we stayed for three years. Dale was born at Ft. Carson just south of Colorado Springs. I left the Air Force and we left the Academy in 1963 and moved to Southern California.

The remaining 4 poems of this section are my anniversary sentiments for each year.

<u>Precious Time</u>
July 2, 1960

Time travels quickly on
In many subtle ways
    The necessary family tasks
    The children, housework, neighbors all
    The friends and relatives that call
    The TV set and telephone
All sap that basic entity
And leave us but a little left
With which to meditate

But even though our time
Seems wasted more than not
    Accomplishments we do achieve
    In more than simple household things
    Or mere scholastic offerings
    Or tangibles that soon decay
We've learned to raise a family
To love and live in harmony
Our precious time well spent

Eighth Anniversary
July 2, 1961

What does it mean a man
His wife to be?
    A family full of brimming boys
    A girl so lovely like herself
    Her mother is –
It means to me

What does it mean a man
His wife to be?
    A house of homes, a living place
    That wears a joy reflecting so
    The likes of her
It means to me

What does it mean a man
His wife to be?
    A night so close and giving
    Dressed in passion free and filled with all
    The love of her
It means to me

What does it mean a man
His wife to be?
    A wondrous beauty deep and deep
    A burning pride that one like her
    His wife would be
It means to me

Nine Years, Life
July 2, 1962

When I think upon my wife
      Her warmth betakes me
            Causing me to blush within

When I look upon my wife
      Her image pleases me
            More beautiful each year

When together she and I
      Two as one
            We know our love

Tenth Anniversary
July 2, 1963

Love is every day
Undercurrents life and death
Bonds the fabric day to day
A word, a glance, a baby's breath

Love is ever there
Lingers in expectancy
Chills in sorrow's random air
Peaks in ecstasy

SPIRITUAL I

This includes poems, eight in all, on loss, death, religion and God that I wrote during the period up to 1963: Tucson, Cleveland, Dayton and Colorado. The category of Spiritual in Book II contains 22 poems, while that of Book III contains 25 poems plus some essays/letters. As we have entered our senior years this category has become increasingly more prevalent.

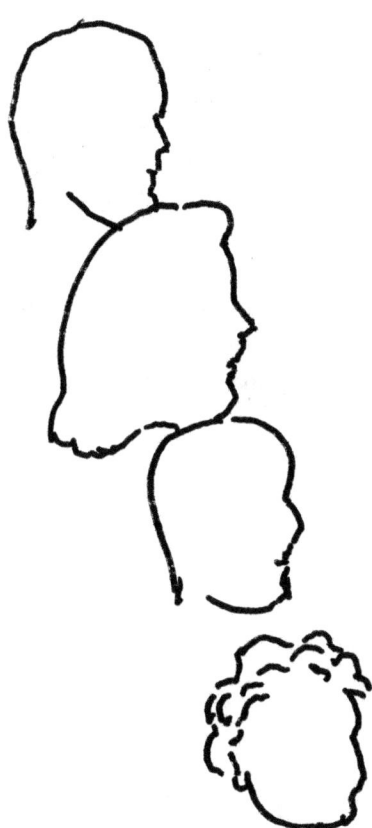

It is easy to be presumptuous about people, thinking that you really know them. We tend to see each as a conglomerate of our personal stereotypes. I am doubtful that it is possible really to know another person completely, even after many years of living together. The poem, Jester, was written in response to my having blatantly experienced this failing in myself.

<u>Jester</u>
Circa 1953 DAC

I met a man who jested much
Of marriage, sex and matters such
Amused, I curiously inquired
If wedlock had this jest inspired

"Yes, I was married for a while –
The Good Lord took my wife and child –
Ah, yes, He should have taken me"
And then continued jesting, he

I can hazily recall the circumstances that prompted the poem, The Dance. Upon reading it I can still feel the emotions, the sense of anger and cynicism that I felt when I wrote it. I believe that I was on a flight to Miami, Florida to meet Marvin, who was flying in from Tucson. The two of us were to locate our father and accompany him back to Tucson.

<u>The Dance</u>
Circa 1957

This is the dance
The stream
The life blood of man
    Listen to the drum beat
    Listen to the drum beat
    Dip and swirl and
    Round and round and
    Rise to the heavens and fall to the ground
Dance to the weak ones
Dance to the blind
Dance to the passions that rob man's mind
    Leap to the leper
    And circle 'round the whore
    Bow to the Devil
    And curtsy to the Lord
We are the wise
    The bold
    The fierce
    The ones who contrive
    To be hobbled half alive ...
        Accuse
        Abuse
        Amuse
        Confuse ...

As an introduction to the poem, To Lisa Ann, a Lullaby, on page 36, I spoke of a fellow officer, whose baby daughter, Maria, had leukemia; and that the two of us formed the Pikes Peak chapter of the Leukemia Society. When Maria died I wrote her the following tribute.

The second poem honors Cynthia, another child in Colorado Springs who died a month or so later.

<u>A Tribute to Maria C</u>
Died of Leukemia
April 8, 1962

A tribute to thine infant rest
Thy holy sacrament

Inspired by thy tender breast
A living monument

For we, in witness of Himself
Who called upon thy name

Resolve that others like thyself
Shall suffer not the same

A Tribute to Cynthia P
Died of Leukemia
May 28, 1962

The heart of Cynthia was strong
Her lovely features did bespeak
Her soul rejoined its Lord ere long
Her vital blood too weak

The sorrow laden parent's brow,
Too soon – too late to harvest grief,
May gather solace in Him now
In merciful relief

We ne'er can help her draw her breath
Restore her precious kindled flame
But band we can to combat death
In honor of her name

Bill was active in the chapter's efforts to raise funds for Leukemia research. He died suddenly of a heart attack.

Bill L.
August 9, 1962

The *kadish* cup is filled with tears
A man has served his span of years
And passed
A mitzvah was his daily bread
He walked the paths where greatness led
His life for life. His memory
Be blessed

Major B had leukemia, was in remission for some years and had recently come out of remission. Even so, he continued his work at the AF Academy and on the chapter's activities.

<u>In Memory of Major B</u>
December 19, 1962 DAC

It was the measure of the man
That he could face his day-to-day
Before his God and fellow man
Full knowing

The wings of courage soar to heights
Unfathomed in the day-to-day
In he who with his life-blood fights
Leukemia

I don't recall the circumstances of this next poem. I believe that Mrs. K was a member of the Colorado Springs synagogue (in which Phyllis and I were active) and that a dear relative of hers had died.

<u>But Memory</u>
To Mrs. K, 1963

What makes the flow of years
    As meted out in smiles and tears
So synthesize our cherished time
    For those whose lives we deem sublime
    But Memory

What makes each moment's fill
    Blessed through years of living, still
To crystalize our span of breath
    Our shifting sands of life and death
    But Memory

I think that this next poem was a culminating observation resulting from having witnessed so much death over the prior two years.

<u>Insensitive</u>
Circa 1963

We tend to be insensitive
To pain that's not our own
In pools of shallow sympathy
We stand
It takes a taste of tragedy
Of suffering alone
To know the sorrow of
Another man

COMMENTARY I

When I was a young man, it seemed that everything elicited an opinion or observation, i.e. everything deserved a comment. There are 43 poems in this category, as opposed to 10 poems in COMMENTARY II and 5 poems in COMMENTARY III. Perhaps this means that over the years I had become commented out, less observant, or had a "been there, done that" attitude. Or perhaps I began more fully to realize that many things were beyond written comment by me.

The summer of 1953, when Phyllis and I wed, I was working at Miami Copper Mine.

A Miner
Circa 1953

A miner is a man
  Whose flesh is meshed with steel
His eyes are primed
  With dirt and grime
  And mud beneath his heels
His wit as sharp as
  Drilling bits
His language black as coal
But none so sound
  As underground
A miner knows his soul

This poem, The Gift, refers primarily to charitable gifting.

A Gift
Circa 1954

A gift is fluxion from the heart
Deep rooted in humility
It sanctifies when dear-to-part
And basks in anonymity

D. Allen Cohen

At this stage of my life (1964) I strongly felt a lack of adequate time to do what was necessary, let alone what I desired to do. I also spent time trying to sift facts out of the barrage of inputs I was receiving.

<u>A Year</u>
Circa 1954

A year, it seems, just comes and goes
But where or when we do not know
It's born, it seems, in effigy
A figment of the ordered mind
To mock the actual flow of time

We celebrate, each year, our birth
That accident of passion's bent
That makes of man eternal man
At least in terms of years

We should instead commemorate
Each second – every century
For life's a century in length
From life to death's a second's length

A year, it seems, just comes and goes
But where or when we do not know

<u>Egg in the Shell</u>
(Humpty Dumpty)
Circa 1954

Fact and fancy, scholarly fun
Fact and fancy rolled into one
Many an hour a man will depart
Foolishly trying to tell them apart

It always thrilled me to be flying at sunset. The world takes on the mantle of dusk, a time when fantasy rules.

Flying Daylight into Dusk
Circa 1954 DAC

A carpet spreads before me
Of blue cast 'round on white
The sun of day fails now this snowy bird
High in the sky
Only blue
Blue on white
Slowly giving way to gray

A glacier looms ahead
Churning violent its vapor fluff
In patterns foaming
Forming always new
Yet somehow
Still unchanged

Gray is deepening to black
And only speckled patches, strata
Can be seen
A hint of light but ever fading
Earth is turning
Motors churning

Now an earthly star appears
And fades
And reappears in multiplicity untold
The lights of darkness wake from daytime slumber
Weaving patterns
Seen in patches
Through the threadbare segments of the carpet
Black on black

Stars of heaven
Star of Earth
Great galactic speck of dust
Nations crumble
Motors rumble
Flying daylight into dusk

Being a father brings back youthful memories. I don't recall which boy was at the origin of this poem, but I can guess.

<u>Glimpse of Memory</u>
Circa 1954

The ostentatious wind of youth
Has ruffled hair and blurred my eyes
Uprooting those complacent truths –
Those well-adjusted lullabies –
And forced me now to look again
Undim my eyes, recall,... recall
The vision of a boy who then
Was ostentatious most of all

The lost and never yesterday
Of years before, of moments past
Unsheathed in sharp reality –
The boy who grew too smart too fast
Where now I stand in judgment of
A boy who mirrors much of me
Un-tempered steel – the image of
A fleeting glimpse of memory

My father was a hobo during his early manhood at the time of the Great Depression. He told many a marvelous story of his hobo-hood. Years later Phyllis gifted me a hollow, rubber hobo doll that reminded me of Dad and his stories. We named the doll, Mr. Bumpkin.

Mr. Bumpkin
To Dad
Circa 1954

In the land of past and pardon
By some vague cerebral garden
    Lives a noble
    Happy hobo
Mr. Bumpkin is his name

He lives not by rote convention
Prompting some remote intention
    He will light the hobo fires
    In the place of my desires
Calling me to go a tramping

The following group of poems either is from Patches or around that time period. They are observations, comments, witticisms and what have you.

<u>Retort</u>, Circa 1954

Be quick to reply
To those who would cry
    "Rearm us –
    They'll harm us –
    We'll die!"
"Tis folly to win by greater the sin"
Just say it ---
They'll spit in your eye!

<u>An Inquiry Into The Inner Workings of Human Emotions</u>
Patches, 1956

Did you ever feel within you
A certain urge to bite
Did you ever feel
Your brain would reel
But there's no one there to fight
    Your mind a seething boil
    Your head a dizzy whirl
Your blood wells up within you
Driving all but RED from sight

Did you ever bellow phrases
Not caring what you say
Did you ever tell to go to hell
And curse the gods away

Then afterword you feel the shame
And wonder what was all to blame ...
It's normal

Axiom
Patches, 1956

I would like to postulate
For reference at some future date
An axiom to regulate
The presence of one's excess weight
    When one's rations palliations
    Amplify one's estimations
    To a point of recreation
    Past one's stomach's expectation
One immediately concludes
That that's the time to terminate

Free Flow of Thought
Patches, 1956

Free flow of thought
    From concentration
Uplifting minds
    A rare sensation
Nebulous spark
    Mental elation
Free flow of thought
    From concentration

Concept of Self
Patches, 1956

How, then, do I exist?
If I were mute of all external sense
Such that no sight – nor sound – nor touch would I perceive
Could this existence be?

And now assume another man
A you who could myself
Ascribe to your intelligence
Would I through your external sense exist?

Then, let us combine ourselves
Where thing and nothing hand in hand
Betake our mortal mind
And lead us to an abyssal dilemma

How would I know my eyes are blue
Without a mirror imaged hue
Or I perceptual thoughts behold
Without the words to use as molds

Both entity and nonety am I
For that that cannot see – nor touch – nor hear
Will live in mute potentiality
When that that I call I has ceased to be

My Perfect Treasure
Patches, 1956

Through centuries so many men have fought
A hundred thousand nameless elements
With vigilance in search of treasure's scent,
The riches that in vain their hearts have sought

These treasures once revealed brought not but grief
To those who thought the world they would obtain
I, too, have sought but search not I in vain
For I have found pure gold in my belief

My treasure freely shared will ne'er deplete
When hoarded it will soon reduce to naught
Used by poor, it makes their wealth complete
Shunned by rich, their riches soon are not

The purest and by far the most worthwhile
My perfect treasure, but a little smile

I would conjecture that most young college students who study late at night might think of themselves as in this next poem.

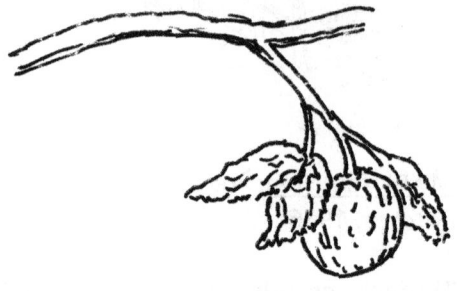

Nocturnal Fruit
Patches, 1956

Tis night
With darkness
Quietude
The din of day relaxes
And the multitude recline in slumber

Yet, some few like me remain to thrash their thoughts
With clearer mind
And dwell on problems yet unsolved
To search for fruit that only
Grows at night

<u>Reality</u>
Patches 1956

Is beauty daughter of the human mind
To shower it with fantasies of truth
Is color color to the color blind
And knowledge knowledge to the tiny youth
      The sky is blue, is blue, is blue
      The grass is green, is green
      And one plus one is two, is two
And so forth --------------
      Now Man views Earth –
      Where fluffy clouds with sails of white
      In azure skies drift out of sight
      And pastures green and sunsets bright
      And starry scenes in summer nights
But what he sees is true only to him
For to each brain there is a world unique
A world that changes with each thought and whim
And never does it know reality
      Yet ----------------------
Electrons circumscribe their nuclei
And oscillations ripple waves through air
And photon waves illuminate the sky
And Grandma sits a-rocking in her chair

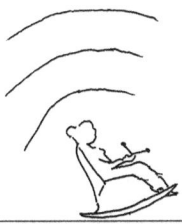

<u>Relativity of Reason</u>
Patches, 1956

Is Justice absolute as such
Too high to touch
The mundane quality
Of man's unique reality

Or is Right relative to man
In that he can
But judge in introspect
With his own variable intellect

Snap Shot
Patches, 1956

Light rays strike a flimsy plate
To image there a spark of time
An instant out of life's design
Its memory to celebrate

The Little Man
Patches, 1956

There's a little man
With a hairy face
He's there within us all
A wide forehead
A pointed chin
And a tail that's half as tall
But what the hell
With a little paint
And a brush to spread it thick
You could never tell
He's down in there
That is – if the paint will stick

The Little Red Ball
Patches, 1956

There's a little red ball
In the middle of the sea
That bobs up and down all day

It's a sly little thing
'Cause the closer you get
The farther it moves away

So you hop in a ship
With a rise and a dip
And a rise and a dip
And a rise and a dip

And just when it's almost within your grip
It's bobbing in some distant bay

The poem, The Little Things, resulted from my being upset with a member of the family who, in my opinion, unintentionally slighted me, lacking sensitivity. In my pique I wrote the poem.

<u>The Little Things</u>
Patches, 1956

The little things it seems
Are the things that pass us by
In the eddies of an instant
Where memories meet fears
Only little things can happen
Little things that pass us by
How little is
    A tear, a laugh, a photograph
    A baby's first-cut tooth
    A song, a dance, the first romance
    The clumsiness of youth
    A worker weary from his toil
    A student going through school
    The son that died on foreign soil
    This life of April Fool
And to look upon this life
    When we laugh
    When we cry
    When we're born
    When we die
It's a little thing that happened
Little things that pass us by

Three Observations
Patches, 1956

The Ant and the Earth

I am so vastly small
All my troubles, worries, cares
Gigantic though they be
Are smaller yet than me

Maturity

A man is wise beyond his years
If he, his past, can counter weigh
To pattern forth his future years
And still live mainly for today

Tissue Paper

We build our bricks of ego high
By looking down on passers by

In my sophomore year at the U of A I became friends with Scott G. He and I would trade verses to see who could write the most cynical refrains. "We Welcome You" was about as far as I would go. I believe that Scott won the contest.

<u>We Welcome You</u>
Circa 1952
Patches

We of the World, we welcome you
To put a label on your head
And stamp it as we choose

To burn within your brain
The mold of our hypocrisy
Until you've learned to stamp and brand as we

D. Allen Cohen

Being away from home, Tucson, for an extended period, I did, now and then get a little homesick. I think that the poem, "A Letter" was the result of one of those periods.

<u>A Letter</u>
Circa 1957

Often in one's daily grind
One neglects to keep in mind
   Other faces
   Other places
Distant not in thought but land
Though one's worries, thoughts and scurries
Does one's precious time demand
One could span the distant miles
In an instant – if one might
Take the pen and start to write
Once – a letter – in a while

I recall writing this next poem, but I can't recall to whom it was referring. My current thinking is that it was Nicki, who as a two-year-old was wide-eyed, uncritically taking in the world around her.

<u>A Virgin Mind</u>
Circa 1957

That tidal flow of salty sea
That washes grains of memory
Like sands of thought upon the beach
Has found a virgin mind to teach

Ho, laugh you worldly winds so cold
Who've toyed with myriad minds of old
Though boldly did you lash their tongues
Tread softly on this one so young

My graduate study was on theoretical physics, including quantum mechanics. Quantum mechanics represents physical reality in terms of a wave function usually referred to as ψ (psi).

ψ

Apologies to E.A. Poe
Circa 1957

Contemplating quantum theory
I had cause to pause and worry
What the meaning
So intriguing
Of this function waving o'er

Lost in physical exploring
Through the lore my mind is pouring
Over deft symbolic scoring
Scoring on the pad before

Tis but ψ and nothing more?

Wrapped in anxious imperceptions
Floundering in vague reflections
Chained to channels
Mental molding
Holding back the meaning o'er

Suddenly in great elation
Came a dawning realization
Most profound in revelation
Laying bare the meaning's core

Tis but ψ and nothing more!

The Laws of the Land
Circa 1957

Deep in the dust of society
Hewn by the mightiest hand
Stands there a structure that's gray with antiquity
Stands there the Laws of the Land

Formed from the fiber of suffering
Tempered by long precedent
Structured and strained by its ages of weathering
Stressed by the world's temperament

Cold though its girders and buttresses
Steeped in tradition's demand
Warmth there abides in its fountains and terraces –
Molding of justice by man

The Scientist
Circa 1957

The world to us a question mark
The realm of symbols we embrace
Abstracting models, we embark
A thread of Nature, there to trace

These models, barren of themselves,
When patterned just for symbol's sake
Give birth to science when they delve
The fundamental laws we make

We make our laws a mockery
Of Nature's subtle symmetry
But in this vague hypocrisy
Lay shadows of reality

This Modern Age
Circa 1957

A way of life
This modern age
Is not a matter for the mind
To weigh each aspect carefully
And thus delineate a plan
It is instead
Determined by
The mass barrage of emptiness
That emanates from every source
Of day to day endeavor

Nor are the passions
(So conceived
To be man's highest vibrancy)
Allowed to culture of themselves
Toward excellence in ecstasy
They dwell instead
With hobbled limbs
In chains of vain morality
Symbolic sensuality
And smutty little rhymes

Where is the man
This modern age
Who dares defy this atrophy
This mass hypnotic tendency
Of mental masturbation
Is he afraid
The timid soul
To be the individual man
To face this fearsome juggernaut
And turn the damn thing off!

A Question, Sirs
Circa 1958

A question let me ask of all who hear
And then let those who care to answer
Come within and join discussion's round
For here we seek no problems to be solved
And neatly placed aside for action at some later date
We thrash our puny minds instead
At only those that have no real results

> Where mere opinion boldly laid
> By those who know of it the least
> Are taken close to heart by all
> As true – how true – so true – quite so!

So hear me then a question, if you please
And if you are of such a mind
To join non-entities like us
In our poor mental ramblings

> Then do come in
> A question sirs:

The Voice of Violins
Circa 1958 DAC

The voice of violins rejoice
In gay and tumbling melodies
The ribboned music leaves its source
And dances sprightly through the air
Seducing each encounter there
To join its sonic intercourse
And tumble with its melodies
In voice as violins rejoice

The voice of violins in force
Triumphant in their melodies
The bannered music leaves its source
And prances regally through air
Inducing each encounter there
To join in colonnades its course
And lift its bannered melodies
In voice with violins in force

The voice of violins remorse
In subtle minor melodies
The laden music leaves its source
And softly permeates the air
Inviting each encounter there
To join its sweet and saddened course
And linger with its melodies
In voice as violins remorse

Toby M was my Grandma Ella's second husband. By trade he drafted fantastic, three-dimensional, precise drawings of mechanical mechanisms for manufacturing firms. To me, more importantly, he was an artist (highly accurate and detailed oil paintings of landscapes) and an inventor (he invented the octagonal, red STOP traffic sign among other things). Toby also had religious and political dream-visions some of which he put to canvas. I was moved to write poems describing two of his painted visions.

The Vision of Toby Miller
Circa 1959

Three vultures I saw there
On flimsy splintered fences
Croaked and peered each other's stare
With wayward glances

And strewn around the waste
Was deadened, leafy foliage
Remnants of a tree's embrace
With nature's spoilage

An old man I saw there
Of Maccabean stature
A Husky beard and blood red hair
A man of nature

He beckoned me to watch
As men approached a buzzard
Drew their knives of bloody blotch
And slit its gizzard

As blood soaked in the sand
The buzzard's boundary vanished
Leaving only barren land
Where hope was banished

Two feather birds remained
Their hooded gazes sneering
Perched on boundaries self-ordained
Each other fearing

The old man signaled me
To leave without returning
But this vision I still see
My memory burning

<u>The Night is Long</u>
Based on a Toby Miller painting:
"Watchman, What of the Night"
Circa 1959

Where led that fervent pious path?
A misty city in the sky
That pinnacled impoverished eyes
And blinded them, its bloody path
      The buzzard's beak
      Is sharp and strong
      Its cry is bleak
      The Night is long
      The Night is long

Ah, Thinker, one of earthy past
Your back is turned on Marble Town
And wearily your eyes look down –

Prepare you for the Sabbath fast?
    A pact o'er blood
    The vulture's song
    Of vanquished mud
    The Night is long
    The Night is long

Can justice balance hell with hell
The mortar blasts and fiery tomb
Against the awful fission bomb
And not with vehemence rebel
    The fertile seed
    Where fruit belongs
    Is parched by deed
    The Night is long
    The Night is long

Ah, Thinker, go you back to earth
And dabble not with nature's might
For man destroys himself by night
And blackens out the germ of birth
    A child draws nigh
    A flame too strong
    And blinds his eye
    The Night is long
    The Night is long

A covenant was made with Man
That he the Sabbath candles burn
And harken not of war to learn
Then bounteous would be the land
    Until the day
    The Israelite
    In peace may pray
    There will be night
    There will be night

These next three poems I wrote shortly after arriving at the Air Force Academy. I can't recall clearly what prompted them except they had to do with the active-duty military society and national politics that prevailed at the time.

Hypocrite
Summer, 1960

I am the hypocrite of old
I think but do as I am told
And when I die my story told
He thought, but did as he was told

War Mongering
Summer, 1960

Our lives are born of tempest times
A seething world of master minds
Who race to sound the rattle chimes
Of war

The battle fields have changed to space
And scientists now set the pace
Unlocking stores from Nature's grace
For war

I Walk the Carpets
October, 1960

I walk the carpets new
    But quaint
My hour in life is strong
    But faint
My rationale is quite
    Unclear
I walk in peace though
    Couched in fear
I see the world with
    Eyes so blind
I grasp at thoughts I
    Never find
And were I dead, as
    Dead I be
I'd live to see
    Eternity

Life's Amenities
Circa 1960

How do we learn of life's amenities
    Of social grace
    Of heart compassionate
Where do we taste of life's nobilities
    Of stately grace
    Of wisdom infinite
When do we feel of life's humilities
    Of silent grace
    Of spirit reverent

We understand the worth of these
On witnessing the dearth of these

After having born Dale, Phyllis was in the Fort Carson military hospital (a group of WWII Quonset huts) for nearly a week. During that time I became the principal parent responsible for Nicki, Mark and Lee.

<u>So Gather Me My Children Round</u>
October, 1960

So gather me my children round
Let's frolic 'fore I bed you down
We'll laugh and sing
And play a game
Of rosy-ring —
About the same
As your old dad
When he was, oh,
A little lad
So long ago

Or rather be a story told
Would please the ears of ones so old
As five and three
And also two
Upon my knee,
Bit crowded, true
But pleased I am
My soul re-fed
What? — Time's run by?
Then off to bed!

Earlier, on page 36, I described our Leukemia Society activities. I composed this poem to be used in the fund-raising campaigns.

<u>Leukemia Campaign</u>
Circa 1962 DAC

I am your loved one
Look at me
I am the one you kissed goodnight
Unknowingly
Of what befell – Leukemic

I am your loved one
Hear me now
Out of tomorrow's memory
I cry the pain
Of having passed – Leukemic

I am your loved one
Win for me
Rally to my memorial plea
That yours may live
I pray thee give – Leukemic

Dr. Josephs was a blind holy man.

>Dr. Josephs
>Circa 1963
>
>He turned his head
>To face my voice –
>Shalom my friend
>My ears rejoice
>I know you well
>
>He spoke the Lord
>And oft did quote
>The Bible's word
>He knew by rote
>A wise Hillel
>
>Unblind thine eyes
>The Old, the New
>And realize
>Your faith anew
>Your faith to be
>
>Then as I rose
>To take my leave
>He held me close
>As though to breathe
>A prayer for me
>
>But please, dear sir
>Pray not for me
>Pray thee for Man
>For I am he
>For I am he

I wrote of my grad-school friend, Marvin B back on page 38. As I recall, at that time of his life he was bitter toward his mother and tended to blame her for his failings. I wrote the following to help him see where he was heading. It would be interesting to compare this with "From Your Son" on page 17.

<u>Mother Loved Me</u>
To Marvin B
Circa 1963

Mother loved me, ' twas her pride
Often when in need I cried
Mother, Mommy be my guide
Mother helped me so I died

Mother caught me when I fell
Kissed away the tears that swell
Sheltered me till I was well
Mother paved my way to hell

Once I took a solo fling
Till the world began to sting
Mother found me floundering
Smothered me beneath her wing

Mother, Mommy dear and true
I owed all my life to you
Where in death I bid adieu
You can take the credit too

After leaving the Air Force and its Academy, we moved to greater Los Angeles.

The City
Los Angeles, Circa 1963

The city
    Horrible, immense
Sprawling grids of gray black mass
    Vision drowning
Smog-brown fingers choking
    Oozing outward
Traffic rivers endless
    Day and night
All within are people
    People, people

EPIC I

    During this period I wrote three, what I label as epic poems: "Song of the Maccabee", "Ode to a Squaw Dress" and "That Mobile Abode". The first two poems were in *Patches,* so they were written prior to 1957 when *Patches* was published. I don't recall just when I wrote "That Mobile Abode", but since the story takes place in the autumn of 1944, I lead off with it here.

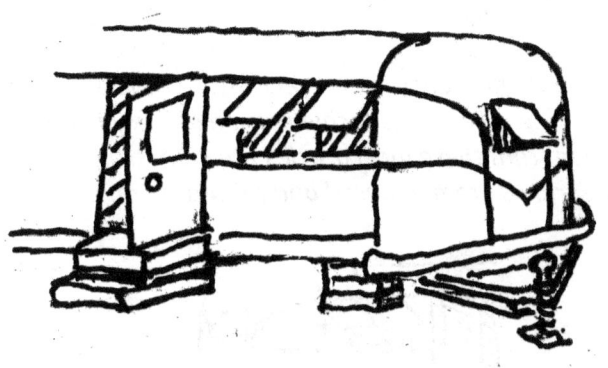

In 1944, Pittsburgh, PA, my mother was told that for medical reasons she had to move to a warm, clean and dry climate like Arizona, and not remain in the then exceedingly dirty atmosphere of that city. "That Mobile Abode" is my recollection fourteen or fifteen years later of the journey to Arizona we, our little family, took. It was during WWII when everything was rationed and one had to have food stamps and gas stamps in order to purchase these items. Also, it was nearly impossible to buy new tires, only re-treads.

I wrote the story in the voice of an eleven-year old and as I recalled it. Marvin, my older brother (12½ at the time) took issue with a few of my "facts". The river-bridge crossing where Faye and Richie were inside the trailer most likely was not the Mississippi, nor was the town where Faye and Richie remained likely in Missouri. However, aside from these inaccuracies the story truly relates the events of the trip as I remembered and relived them.

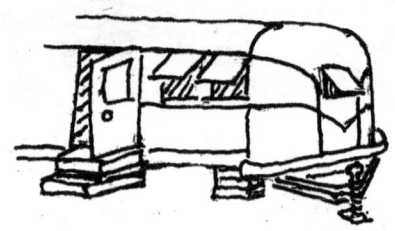

That Mobile Abode
Circa 1957

In early September one fine autumn eve
The Cohens were packed and all ready to leave
In a sixteen-foot trailer from bumper to hitch
And an old black sedan that was ready to ditch.
That quaint little trailer had plenty of room
For the five of us in there and maybe the broom.
The table collapsed to a small double bed,

No water or toilet – a night pail instead.
A coal-burning heater and gasoline stove
With all the convenience of home while we drove.
From Pittsburgh to Tucson was many a mile
But we were excited, at least for a while.
So into the car we all bounded with joy,
My mother and father and three of us boys.
Now Marvin was eldest, twelve years to his name –
Then Allen, eleven, the author's the same,
Then wee little Richie, just thirty-eight weeks –
Our hearts full of hopes and our car full of squeaks.
We dreamed of the desert with skies blue and clear
And pictured the antelope playing with deer,
The Indians with feathers, the cowboys with hats ---
Then ten miles from Pittsburgh we had our first flat.
Alas how the luck had our journey begun
And so was our fortune the rest of the run.
We went on to Akron to bid our adieu
To cousins and uncles and grandparents too.
From there up to Cleveland – goodbye to the rest
And focused our faces on sunny southwest.

We'd drive through the day and as evening would fall
We'd locate a camp and we'd park in a stall.
Now Dad did the parking while we'd guide him through –
First turning, then twisting, then starting anew.
We'd block up the trailer then unhitch the horse
And run for the little rooms – nature, of course.
Mom's voice in the twilight would call out the chores
While Dad would run down to the local food store.
We'd put out the playpen that rode in the trailer
And fire up the coals after numerous failures.
Marvin would pump up the gasoline stove
While I'd fetch the water, a task that I loathed.
We'd tip toe around while setting the table
With delicate balance – it was quite unstable.

D. Allen Cohen

Then just as we'd settle ourselves for the meal
An elbow would blunder and then the ordeal.
One end of the table would fly in the air
Removing the victuals with nary a care
On dresses and trousers and onto the floor.
We'd clean up then practice the ritual once more.
When dishes were done and we all had been fed
We'd be so worn out that we'd just go to bed.

Through Indiana and through Illinois
We sailed like a baby would sail through his toys –
Now crawling, now sitting, now turning around
Now up on all fours and now flat on the ground.
We made it somehow to the old Mississippi
Our spirits were damp and the weather was nippy.
My mother was tired and Richie was hungry.
She wanted to stop but my dad became angry.
"We have to make time so go ride in the trailer
And if it's too rough then just give us a holler."
So Mom and the baby adjourned to the house
And Dad revved the car; we were off with a bounce.
Poor Mom didn't know she was in for a treat
For the car and the bridge hit a resonant beat,
And while we were crossing that lazy old river
The trailer house started to shimmy and shiver.
It seemed to be swaying all over the road
And all hell broke loose in that mobile abode.
The cupboards flew open, the table upset,
The sight was one such that you'd never forget.
The passengers bodily tossed side to side,
But we in the car were enjoying the ride.
Mom grabbed up the baby and screamed herself hoarse
But try as she may, couldn't alter our course.
Once over the river Dad halted to check
And found there my mother a terrified wreck.
Now history was made on that cross-river cruise,

My mother discovered the Saint Louis bruise.

'Twas not after long in some town in Missouri
While creeping along in our natural hurry
When Mom noticed people were staring aghast
And a boy on a bicycle yelled as he passed.
Dad stopped to inspect and beheld in a daze
That a part of our humble abode was ablaze.
He bounded inside after giving a call
And grabbed the extinguisher down from the wall.
He battled his way to the source of the smoke
And smothered the flames – and then started to choke.
But it wasn't the fumes that caused tears to transpire
Nor the cracked axle pin that had prompted the fire –
For the wheel started listing and rubbing the housing
Adjoining a cupboard, the flames there arousing.
'Though Dad saved the trailer and no one was hurt
My father had lost his best dozen white shirts.
Alas my poor mother by then had enough.
From bridges to axles, the trip was too tough.
So she and the baby remained there to rest
And now there were three of us traveling west.

The trip through the Ozarks was pleasant and smooth.
The rolling green hills had the power to soothe
The rumbling racket our motor-car made
Allowing reality gently to fade.
I daydreamt of cowboys and Indians out west –
My stallion was saddled for I was in quest
Of desperate bandits who'd held up the stage.
I leapt to my horse and lit out for the sage.
I tracked them through mountains and valleys of cactus,
Shooting at road signs to keep me in practice,
Until I caught sight of them high on a bluff
Then I moved in slowly for these men were rough.
They spotted me coming and started to fire ---

D. Allen Cohen

Then I drew and BANG! --- another flat tire.

We saw our first Indian in Oklahoma,
A Manhattan suit and a college diploma.
His only feather was in his hat
And he passed us up in a Cadillac.
In Texas we got our first glimpse of a cowhand,
Levies and boots and a faded red neckband,
A dirty old Stetson that brought him his luck
And he rode the range in a pickup truck.
The days seemed long and the road stretched far
Out there in the state of the lonesome star.
And many's the time we would run out of water
But somehow we reached the New Mexican border.
As low as our luck might have been before
It was here that it finally hit the floor.

About twelve miles short of Tucumcari
A two-horse town in the midst of prairie
The pin that supported the left trailer wheel
Gave way like the other, the former ordeal.
We parked the abode by an old ranch site
And drove to the village to spend the night.
The following morning we canvassed the shops;
We scouted the alleys and queried the cops.
We turned the town over but to our chagrin
There wasn't the trace of an axle pin.
But Lady Luck smiled with a cursory glance;
We spotted the shop of a blacksmith by chance –
An anvil and hammer, a kiln and of course
The jolly old smith who was shoeing a horse.
On hearing the tale of our axle-pin plight
He said he could forge one to do the job right.
Some time would be needed to grind it the same
And Dad had but few dollars left to his name.
He then wrote a letter to Mom in Missouri

And asked her to wire some cash in a hurry.
The letter was somehow misplaced and not mailed.
We waited for money but to no avail.
One evening soon after Dad said with a smile
"Tomorrow we all go to work for a while."
The news was exciting in spite of our woe.
We supped and then spent our last buck on a show.

At four the next morning Dad woke us from sleep.
We dressed and then piled in our rackety heap
And drove to the center of Tucumcari
Awaiting a truck that was going to carry
The three of us out to some destination
To labor the day for our next week's rations.
The wind was cold as the pale moon shone
And I felt a shiver that chilled my bones.
Before very long as the night turned gray
The truck came along and we rumbled away.
Within were seated a group of people –
The young, the strong, the aged and feeble,
Mexicans, Indians, women and men –
They numbered, I think, about nine or ten.
Strewn on the bed of the truck was a bunch
Of watermelons to serve for lunch.
A tarpaulin covered us overhead
And the road fell back like a wrinkled thread.
We traveled for maybe an hour or more
With never a mention of what was in store.
We finally stopped with a squeak and a jerk
And Dad gave a wink with a sly little smirk.
"Well boys, you will wish you had never been born
After spending the day picking ripe broom corn."
Now broom corn's the stuff out of which you make brooms.
It grows in a stalk and you harvest the bloom.
Secured to a staff it may well sweep your floor
But I'll never want to pick brooms anymore.

D. Allen Cohen

We worked through the morning 'till lunch came around
Then each grabbed a melon and sat on the ground.
We gorged ourselves silly with water and pulp,
Spitting the seeds out between every gulp.
My father then joined in a nobler sport –
Those six-sided bones that brought cursing retorts
From the men, as my father adept with the dice,
Started winning the loot. 'Twas enough to suffice
Us the rest of the time 'till the pin was all made,
Allowing the labor and parts to be paid.
My mother and Richie were still in Missouri.
Not hearing from us she became very worried
And called the New Mexican Highway Patrol
To locate our bodies and tally the toll.
For Mom had envisioned the three of us dead
In some hidden canyon where paths never led.
Her neighbors, of course, tried to soothe all her fears
And told her that finding us may take a year.
But finally mail brought her fears to an end
And soon we were all back together again.
Then Tucumcari became our home
At least 'till we could afford to roam.
To school again went my brother and I;
My father found work and the autumn rolled by.

Some time around then we became good friends
With an old ranch hand who would often lend
Us a quarter horse, an old white mare
With saddle and blanket and bridle to wear.
Before very long my brother and I
Were riding like cowboys, sombreros held high,
Both feet in the stirrups, a hand on the reigns,
Our hearts full of thunder, our thighs full of pains.
Then came the big day, the day of the year,
The day that the rodeo swung into gear.
The cowboys flocked in from out on the prairie

To vie at the fairgrounds in Tucumcari.
My brother and I rode the old white mare
And joined many others to watch the affair.
The cowboys were decked in their brightest of shirts;
Their horses were restless, their nostrils alert.
Excitement rode high as the crowds filled the stands
And everyone cheered as the boss raised his hand.
The grand march was on and the colors rode by
The dust from the hoof beats enveloped the sky.
Then history dressed in tradition's array
Re-enacted itself on that rodeo day.
Each event bore a symbol of vigorous past
When a cowboy was tough and his pony was fast.
These time honored contests, these noblest of duels
Of man against beast, of brave against bull –
Calf roping, bull dogging, and tricky team tying,
Brahma bull, bare-back and saddle-bronc riding –
The clowns, the trick riders, the cowboys and all,
It made the most wondrous of days to recall.

Soon into winter the weather turned fowl.
The wind on our window would whistle and howl.
The snow started falling; the sky turned to gray
And I turned to bedside to fever away.
'Twas late in December before we resumed
The journey that started one fall afternoon.
And though we were weary our spirits were high.
We joked and sang songs as the miles rolled by.
We cheered as New Mexico passed out of view
And into the land of saguaro we flew.
Up through the pine covered mountains we steered
And watched while the antelope played with the deer.
Then down into desert and out 'cross the plains
And into the land of the never-fall rains –
The blue skies and sunsets that welcome your heart,
The good land of Tucson, a new life to start.

Early in 1950, while still living in a trailer (a larger one by then) in the same trailer court on Oracle road as when we first arrived in Tucson, my mother started designing and making western style patio aprons. She organized the women in the court that had sewing machines such that the court became her factory. She called the business "Faye Creations". The business grew as she branched into colorful, western-style dresses, then called "squaw dresses". As the business expanded, my father joined and took over sales; they leased a spacious building not far from Saint Mary's hospital in Tucson and outfitted it for the business. In order to achieve all this they took on a "silent" partner, Mr. G who factored the finances. I was a student at the U of A at the time and I worked part time at the factory. During that period I wrote "Ode to a Squaw Dress".

Ode to a Squaw Dress
Patches, 1953

Wake up in the morning
Jump out of bed
Pull my squaw dress
Over my head
Sprinkle my face

Mess with my hair
Gulp down some Postum
No time to spare
Send little Richie
Off to his school
"Listen to teachers!
Obey the rules!"
Honk, there's the car
Now off to the shop
Cannot be late
Production will stop.

"Good morning girls,
Get back to your job!"
    "The machines out of order
    The bobbins won't bob,
    The stitches won't stitch,
    They won't feed the threads,
    The belts are too loose,
    You need new heads!"
"All right! All right!
I'll call a mechanic.
Hello? Come out!
My shop is a panic!
My bobbins won't bob,
They won't feed the threads,
My stitches won't stitch.
I need a new head!"

I hope, at least, the cutting's been done.
"For heaven's sake
You've just begun!"
      Well Ma'am your Partner
      Said we were wrong;
      The twelves look like tens,
      And the tens are too long."
"The tens are too long?!"
      "And the twelves look like tens."
"I'd better size them over again."
Hm-mm tens are okay
Twelves are too
There's someone's ear
I'm going to chew

"Good morning Sir!"
      "'Morning (puff)"
"I - "
      "Where are the blouses?!
      "Let's get out this stuff!"
"Now just a min - (cough!)
      "See what **I** mean (puff)
      There's only one way
      To clean a latrine (puff)
      Must use lye (puff)
      Plenty of spray ---"
And so on and so forth
      Through most of the day (whew)

Now let's see
What dresses to pack.
There must be hundreds
Still on the rack!
"What's holding up shipment
On this batch?"
    "Well, Ma'am, the orders
    And dresses don't match."
"In just a minute I'll give you hand."
I can't see why they don't understand.
"This order's from 'Midlins
Is ready to go
Except for 'two-thirtys'
Material is low.
And so we will pull some
From 'Georgess'
A twelve and an eight,
Or should we save theirs,
Their shipment is late.
Oh well, we'll take
From 'Junior Miss',
But they didn't order
A style like this.
Now what was scheduled
For them, anyway - ?
A skirt in yellow,

A blouse in gray
With ball fringe
Spiraling up the waste,
And foam-rubber cups
That are pleated to taste"
    "But, Ma'am, I shipped that
    In yesterday's mail!
    It wasn't marked special
    So how could I tell?"

"Now here are two dresses
Whose braid doesn't match.
This garment belongs
To yesterday's batch.
I don't understand
How you missed the braid
Although the pattern's
Identically made,
The warps and the woofs -
Look closely here! —
Are opposite.
You see? Quite clear!
But I don't know
I fret and strain
And beat my fists
And wrack my brain
And stomp and storm
And cry and fight
And get no sleep
Throughout the night
All just to get
The dresses made -
And YOU match up
The WRONG braid!!"

    Well, maybe the pleating
    Is going all right.
    "How many skirts
    Are left for tonight?"
        "Well, Ma'am, there's
        Seventy-nine not done."
    "You mean you've only
    Completed ONE?!!"
        "Well, Ma'am, my finger,
        It got a prick
        And I started feeling
        A little sick -
        So I was just
        Going in to lie down
        When just then I got
        A phone call from town -
        My dearest neighbor
        Three blocks away
        Was found in bed
        And dead, they say.
        The funeral's tomorrow
        I'd sure like to go!"
    On this type of thing
    One shouldn't say no.

Five thirty finally
Rolls around
I lock the doors
And windows down
I stagger home
And eat some food
"You know this food
Is very good.
The pie you baked
Just can't be beat
But I'm just too
Darn tired to eat."

Finally Richie's
Fast asleep
And Allen has
 Some date to keep
And Marvin's studying
Out at Don's
I think I'll turn
Some music on.

Ahh, this is nice
To lie in bed
And feel the pillow
Against my head –
I just got
A great sensation
For a brand new

<u>Faye</u> Creation-
Where's my ric-rac?
Where's my braid?
Where's the pattern
I just made?

Oh well,
This new idea will keep
I think that I'll
Just go to sleep.

At the U of A both Marvin and I were active with the university's chapter of the Hillel Society for Jewish Students. Marvin was an officer and I led the group that produced the chapter's newspaper. For the 1952 Hillel celebration of the Jewish holiday, Chanukah, I composed and sang the following song that tells the story of Chanukah.

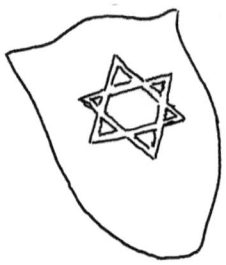

The Song of the Maccabee
Patches, 1952

I sing this song of a priest of old
And five bold sons had he
The bravest and strongest of all his sons
Was Judah Maccabee, Maccabee
Was Judah Maccabee

It was many, many long years ago
In one sixty five BCE
When the Temple atop of Moriah fell waste
By Assyrian companies, companies
By Assyrian companies

Then messengers went throughout the land
Bearing a foreign decree
That all the Jews must renounce their Lord
Or pay the great penalty, penalty
Or pay the great penalty

When a messenger came unto Modin
The town of the Maccabee
Mattathias, the priest of old
Struck the messenger down to his knees, his knees
Stuck the messenger down to his knees

Then Mattathias turned to the crowd
And shouted to them this plea
That all you sons of Israel
Come join and follow me, follow me
Come join and follow me

Mattathias took to the hills
And many a battle fought he
Until one day he was wounded full score
Now he lives on in memory, memory
Now he lives on in memory

Then Judah, son of the priest of old
The one called the Maccabee
Led all the sons of Israel
To their greatest victory, victory
To their greatest victory

The Temple atop of Moriah restored
Restored by the Maccabee
And all Jerusalem celebrates
That Israel is free, is free
That Israel is free

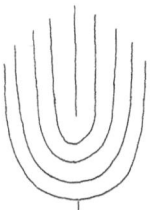

INTRODUCTION TO BOOK II, THE MIDDLE YEARS
1964 TO 1999

In 1963 we left the Air Force and its academy and moved to Santa Ana, California. We lived there until 1968 whereupon we moved to Israel, living most of the time in Rehovot. In 1973 we moved back to the US and took up residence in Long Beach, California. Then in 1982 we relocated to Vienna, Virginia.

One thread that ran through much of this period is in the person of Rabbi Reuven B and his family. This was a highly communal period in our life encompassing community activities and many wonderful friends, with many of whom we remain in contact. However, foremost in our lives during this period was the growth of our family, marriages, grandchildren and wonderful family experiences. This is reflected under the category of "Occasions II" containing 48 poems. My increased interest in spirituality and religion is witnessed by the 22 poems in that category. "My Love II", containing 16 poems, gives testimony to our ever maturing and deepening relationship. Also, as seen by the 10 poems in the "Commentary II" category I have become somewhat less vocal and, exhibit perhaps greater depth in my observations. "Epics II" features the adventures of Pa Poke plus a blow-by-blow account of our China tour and the "Song of the Maasai" out of Africa.

INTRODUCTION TO BOOK III, THE LATER YEARS
2000 TO 2013

The later years occur in Virginia (until 2003), San Jose, Baja Sur California, Mexico (several months at a time) and Tucson, Arizona (since 2003).

Our life has been occupied with many happy occasions, 108 poems in that category such that we feel truly blessed. However, many deaths of family and friends have also occurred. Twenty six mostly difficult-to-write poems are in the "Spiritual III" category. Presuming that I write our 60th anniversary poem in time for this edition, there will be 22 poems in the category of "My Love III". "Commentary III" contains 5 not-so-easy-to-read poems; while I put three rather short epic poems into that category.

Overall both Phyllis and I know that we have been blessed with a marvelous life, sincere friends, and a wonderful, growing, achieving and mutually loving family. Our greatest desire is for this family to remain mutually loving and caring through the generations. This is the ultimate purpose of these three volumes. In the achievement of this goal our blessings will truly be enduring.

www.ingramcontent.com/pod-product-compliance
Lightning Source LLC
Chambersburg PA
CBHW071310060426
42444CB00034B/1762